GW01161469

Original title:
Starry-Eyed Sleepytime

Author: Aurora Sinclair
ISBN HARDBACK: 978-9916-90-736-8
ISBN PAPERBACK: 978-9916-90-737-5

## Quietude in the Heart of the Night

Silent whispers weave the air,
As moonlight bathes the world so fair.
Stars are gems in velvet skies,
Resting dreams with gentle sighs.

Time stands still in night's embrace,
Easing worries, finding grace.
Echoes of the day now fade,
In this peace, our souls are laid.

## Resting Under Astral Wings

Beneath the vast, celestial dome,
Hearts find solace, far from home.
Galaxies swirl, a dance so bright,
Dreamers lost in pure delight.

With every breath, the cosmos sings,
Carrying hopes on starlit wings.
In this moment, all is right,
Wrapped in love, we take our flight.

## Slumberscape of Shimmering Lights

In the stillness, colors blend,
As night unfolds, our worries mend.
Softly glowing, dreams take flight,
In the beauty of the night.

Twinkling paths, we softly tread,
In this slumberscape, we're led.
A canvas bright of dreams anew,
Painting skies in hues of blue.

## When Dreams Wander in the Night

When shadows dance and whispers grow,
Through twilight's veil, our visions flow.
Dreams embark on journeys wide,
With the stars as our guide.

In the realm where night unfolds,
All our stories yet untold.
Mysteries blend with soft moonlight,
As dreams wander through the night.

# Celestial Shadows of Sleep

In twilight's gentle embrace, we lie,
The moon whispers secrets, floating high.
Stars like diamonds in velvet skies,
Guide weary souls to where silence sighs.

Dreams drift softly on night's cool breath,
Carried by shadows, they dance with death.
A lullaby sung by the universe wide,
In celestial realms, we wish to confide.

Lost in the stillness, we find our grace,
In the shadowy corners, a sacred space.
Night unfolds like a soft, chill cloak,
While the world whispers secrets, softly spoke.

Embrace the silence, let worries cease,
In celestial shadows, we find our peace.

## Whispers in the Cosmic Night

Stars scatter secrets across the sky,
Silent whispers float, on dreams they fly.
Galaxies dance in a waltz divine,
While hearts pulse gently, in rhythm and rhyme.

Nebulae cradle hopes long gone,
Echoes of laughter, in starlight drawn.
The vastness hums with stories untold,
In the cosmic night, mysteries unfold.

Time slips softly, like sand in hands,
As we wander through these timeless lands.
Each twinkle a promise, each shadow a sigh,
In the echoes of night, our spirits soar high.

Whispers weave through the fabric of dark,
Kindling the dreams that spark and embark.

## Pillow Prayers for Dreamers

In the hush of night, a prayer takes flight,
Whispered to stars, seeking lost light.
Pillow's soft cradle, where thoughts unfurl,
Hopes held gently, like petals that swirl.

Each sigh a wish, drifting on air,
Carried to heavens, where dreams lay bare.
Closed eyes imagine worlds vast and bright,
Guided by kindness, wrapped in the night.

Figures of comfort dance in our sleep,
Guarding the secrets that we wish to keep.
In slumber's embrace, we chase after grace,
Finding our solace in this sacred space.

Pillow prayers linger, soft and serene,
In the realm of dreams, we're forever keen.

## A Cruise Through Starry Seas

A boat of stardust glides on the night,
Through shimmering waters, ethereal light.
Each wave a whisper, a tale it tells,
Of cosmic creatures where wonder dwells.

Sailing on beams of silver and gold,
Mysteries unfold, though they never grow old.
Dancing through constellations far and wide,
On a cosmic cruise where dreams collide.

Galaxies shimmer like jewels in the dark,
While comets blaze trails, a vivid spark.
Embracing the night, we roam unconfined,
With each gentle swell, we leave cares behind.

A voyage eternal, through space we glide,
On a cruise through the stars, forever our guide.

## Melodies of the Night Sky

Stars shimmer bright in twilight's grace,
Whispers of night in a soft embrace.
The moonlight dances on silver streams,
As dreams take flight on gentle beams.

Harmonies echo through darkened skies,
Mysteries woven in the night's sighs.
Each note a story, each spark a rhyme,
Together they weave the fabric of time.

## Driftwood Dreams in a Celestial Sea

Driftwood floating on a sea of stars,
Whispers of wonders from afar.
The currents of night cradle and sway,
Carrying dreams until break of day.

Each wave a lullaby, soft and sweet,
Gentle reminders of time's heartbeat.
Tides whisper secrets in the moon's light,
Guiding us home through the velvet night.

## Whispers of Moonlit Dreams

In the hush of night where shadows creep,
Dreams unfurl while the world's asleep.
Moonbeams scatter like petals in air,
Inviting hearts to wander and dare.

Whispers of magic in every sigh,
Lifting spirits as they drift by.
In softest moments, the night reveals,
The dreams that the silken darkness conceals.

## Celestial Slumber Serenade

Stars gather round like a velvet choir,
Singing sweet notes that lift us higher.
In the stillness, where dreams unfold,
Stories of wonder and magic told.

With every twinkle, the cosmos hums,
Cradling us softly as twilight comes.
A serenade of peace in the night,
Guiding our dreams till the morning light.

# Crickets Sing to the Milky Way

In fields where shadows play,
The crickets start to sway,
Their songs, a gentle hum,
Beneath the evening's drum.

As stars begin to blink,
The world begins to think,
Each chirp a tale unfolds,
In harmony, it holds.

The Milky Way above,
A ribbon of pure love,
In night's embrace so tight,
Crickets sing in delight.

Underneath this vast dome,
They weave a cosmic home,
In rhythm with the night,
Where dreams take glorious flight.

# Mellow Moods of the Milky Night

The moon's soft velvet glow,
Wraps the world down below,
In gentle whispers, it calls,
While silence gently falls.

Stars twinkle with a smile,
Inviting us a while,
To linger 'neath their light,
In mellow moods of night.

The breeze carries a song,
That feels both sweet and strong,
Each note a warm embrace,
In this enchanted space.

And as the hours creep,
The universe in deep,
Holds secrets we can't know,
In the night's serene flow.

## Hushed Secrets in the Starlit Sky

In the hush of the night,
Stars whisper soft and bright,
Their secrets float like dreams,
In silver-colored beams.

The moon watches in grace,
A tranquil, glowing face,
While constellations weave,
Stories that love believe.

Beneath this cosmic dance,
We find the perfect chance,
To share our hopes and fears,
And glimpse through endless years.

In this vast, quiet space,
We find our rightful place,
With every star a spark,
Illuminating the dark.

## Nebula Nights and Dreamy Sighs

In nebula's embrace,
We drift through time and space,
Each color paints the air,
With wonders beyond compare.

Dreamy sighs intertwine,
Like echoes soft, divine,
In whispers of the night,
We chase the fading light.

Galaxies spin around,
In silence, we are found,
Lost in the starry hues,
With every wish, we choose.

As twilight starts to fade,
And daylight's on parade,
We'll hold onto the sighs,
Of nebula nights and skies.

## The Night's Embrace

In shadows deep, the soft winds sigh,
Wrapped in twilight, the stars drift by.
A whispering hush, the world's asleep,
Cradled in silence, the secrets we keep.

The moonlight dances on silver streams,
Weaving through thoughts, igniting our dreams.
As night unfolds, with magic so bright,
We wander freely, lost in the night.

## Starlit Journey to Dreamland

Beneath a sky of diamond streams,
We sail along on whispered dreams.
Guided by lights that shimmer and glow,
Into the depths where wild dreams flow.

Each star a tale, an ancient song,
Carried by wings, where shadows belong.
Through fields of wonder, our spirits soar,
To dreamland's gate, forevermore.

## Cosmic Embrace of Rest

Wrapped in the cosmos, we find our peace,
As the universe sighs and troubles cease.
Stars hum a lullaby, soft and clear,
Welcoming all who wander near.

In nebula's arms, gently we drift,
Cradled by starlight, a celestial gift.
The endless dark, a comforting place,
Where hearts find solace in night's embrace.

## Glistening Dreams by Moonlight

Moonlight filters through the trees,
A silver cloak in a gentle breeze.
Each twinkle holds a secret deep,
Whispers of magic in dreams we keep.

As shadows play on the velvet ground,
In every heartbeat, wonder is found.
Glistening paths of a tranquil night,
Lead us to dreams bathed in soft light.

## Echoes of Nighttime Bliss

In the hush of night, whispers play,
Stars twinkle softly, lighting the way.
Moonbeams dance on tranquil streams,
Carrying secrets of silent dreams.

Breezes sigh through the ancient trees,
A lullaby sung with gentle ease.
Shadows stretch in the cool night air,
Where peace settles without a care.

## Starlight Spirals of the Soul

Galaxies spin in the heart's embrace,
Each twinkling star a warm, familiar place.
Winding paths of silver light,
Guide us onward through the night.

Auroras dance, a spectral show,
Whispers of wonder in the cosmic flow.
Fates entwined in the twilight glow,
As our spirits soar and gently grow.

## Where Dreams Meet the Cosmos

In the realm where dreams take flight,
Galaxies mingle in the velvet night.
Whispers of hope weave through the air,
Filling the void with love to share.

Nebulas bloom like flowers bright,
Painting the skies with colors of light.
We drift on currents of starlit streams,
Finding solace in our shared dreams.

## Soft Light of the Dreamworld

Gentle hues paint the midnight scene,
As shadows play in a world unseen.
Clouds like pillows float in the sky,
Where worries fade and spirits fly.

The soft light wraps us in warm embrace,
A tender moment, a sacred space.
In this sanctuary, hearts unite,
Beneath the glow of the tranquil night.

## The Gentle Breath of Evening

Whispers glide on the cool night air,
Softly cradling dreams that dare.
The sun bows low, painting skies,
As twilight kisses weary sighs.

Stars awaken with shimmering light,
Guiding lost souls through the night.
Moonbeams dance on silken streams,
While nature hums in velvet dreams.

## Aurora's Gentle Slumber

Morning hues embrace the dawn,
A tapestry where shadows yawn.
Frosted whispers greet the day,
As night slips softly away.

Petals unfold to the warm sun's glow,
Each moment cradles dreams in tow.
Auroras weave in playful grace,
Awakening the world's embrace.

## Fantasies Under the Astral Canopy

Beneath the vast, enchanting sky,
Dreams of stardust gently lie.
Whirls of galaxies intertwine,
In the space where hopes align.

Constellations spin their tales,
In shimmering light, a love prevails.
Fantasies drift like cotton clouds,
Cradled softly without loud crowds.

## Murmurs of the Dreamy Cosmos

In the silence of the endless dark,
Stars breathe softly, leaving a mark.
Murmurs echo from afar,
As dreams align with every star.

Luminous streams of cosmic light,
Guide lost stories through the night.
In this realm where wonders weave,
The heart finds solace and believes.

## Cosmic Caresses on Feathered Clouds

In the cradle of twilight's embrace,
Feathered dreams begin to unfold,
Cosmic whispers touch every face,
As starlit tales of wonder are told.

Gentle breezes in night's caress,
Lifting hearts to celestial heights,
Clouds woven with silvery dress,
Cradle souls beneath the starlit nights.

Galaxies twirl in playful dance,
Painting skies with hues of the rare,
Each twinkle a fleeting romance,
In the realm of the cosmic air.

Bathe in the glow of gentle light,
Feel the magic in every breath,
On feathered clouds take tranquil flight,
Transcending the bounds of life and death.

## Veiled Wonders of Night's Rest

In the quiet of the midnight hour,
Secrets linger beneath the veil,
Mysteries bloom like fragrant flower,
In the silence where dreams set sail.

Moonlight dances on whispered plans,
Casting shadows that softly creep,
Nature sways to a lullaby's bands,
As the world sinks into a deep sleep.

Stars like jewels in velvet spread,
Guard the hush of the cosmos still,
Carrying dreams where hearts are led,
Through the night, they gently will.

Veiled wonders in slumber's embrace,
Unlocking gates to realms untold,
Awakening echoes in time and space,
Where each wish finds the courage to be bold.

## Whispered Secrets Among the Stars

In a sky adorned with light's embrace,
Whispers drift on the cosmic tide,
Secrets shared in a sacred space,
Where galaxies and dreams collide.

Voices echo in starry retreats,
Carried forth on celestial sighs,
In the silence where longing meets,
The tapestry of midnight skies.

Each twinkle a message, a sign,
Bridging the vastness of deep night,
Connecting hearts with threads divine,
Crafting visions that take their flight.

Among the stars, we laugh and cry,
In the warmth of a stellar glow,
Whispered secrets, a cosmic sigh,
Binding souls in the dance below.

## Sailing into Dreamlit Horizons

Set your sails to the winds of night,
Where dreamlit horizons softly call,
Beyond the veil of twilight's light,
In the sea of stars, we rise and fall.

With every wave, let the currents take,
Guiding hearts to shores unknown,
In this voyage, no fear to wake,
For in dreams, we are never alone.

The horizon blends with shades of gold,
As the dawn breaks on a brand new day,
Stories of wonder and courage told,
In the light of hope, we find our way.

Sailing onward, we chase the gleam,
Of worlds beyond our waking eyes,
In the voyage of life, we dare to dream,
Finding solace where the spirit flies.

## Slumber Beneath the Milky Veil

In the hush of night so deep,
Stars weave dreams while others sleep.
Moonlight dances, soft and pale,
Cradling hearts within the veil.

Whispers float on evening's breeze,
Rustling leaves in secret trees.
Beneath the sky, a lullaby,
Cradles gently, time slips by.

Dreamers drift in silken streams,
Caught in the web of tender dreams.
Milky Way, your starlit trail,
Guides us home, where love prevails.

Wrapped in slumber, spirits soar,
Glistening stars, forever more.
In this night, we find our peace,
Underneath the veil, we cease.

## Fantasia of the Drowsy Sky


Clouds like pillows float above,
Embracing dreams, the night we love.
Twilight whispers, soft and low,
Painting shades of indigo.

In this realm where shadows play,
Every moment melts away.
Gentle breezes hum a tune,
Calling forth the silver moon.

Stars begin their graceful dance,
In the dark, they take their chance.
Lazily, the world transforms,
Wrapped in wonder, night conforms.

Time drifts softly, lost in flight,
In this realm of pure delight.
Fantasia breathes a calming sigh,
As we dream beneath the sky.

## Nocturnal Reveries in Indigo

In the stillness, shadows blend,
Nocturnal sights, a dream to send.
Midnight calls with velvet grace,
Inviting us to find our place.

Indigo nights, a canvas fair,
Painted with starlight's gentle flare.
Whispers echo, soft and warm,
In these dreams, we transform.

Mirrors of the moonlit sea,
Reflect our thoughts, wild and free.
Drifting through each fleeting hour,
Lost in night's enchanting power.

Reveries in still embrace,
In warmth of night, we find our space.
Each soft breath, a story told,
In this trance, our souls unfold.

## The Dreamweaver's Nocturne

In twilight's embrace, she weaves her threads,
Stitching visions where silence treads.
A melody hums through the whispering trees,
Carried on the wings of a soft evening breeze.

Each note a promise, each chord a bloom,
Crafting shapes in the fabric of gloom.
With silvered hands, she spins the night,
Creating a tapestry laced with light.

## Floating on a Sea of Starlight

On waves of starlight, we drift and glide,
Cradled by cosmos, in dreams we reside.
Nebulas swirl, painting skies anew,
In this vast ocean, our spirits break through.

Constellations guide us, bright beacons of hope,
Through the infinite dark, we learn how to cope.
Floating gently, we find our way,
In the sea of starlight, forever we'll stay.

## Embrace of the Twilight Goddess

Beneath the gaze of twilight's eye,
The world beneath begins to sigh.
Goddess cloaked in shades of blue,
Calls to hearts, both brave and true.

Her gentle touch, a soothing balm,
Wraps the earth in peace, so calm.
Stars awaken, slowly rise,
Guided by her luminous guise.

In her arms, we find our rest,
Wrapped in dreams, the very best.
Fingers weave through time and space,
In her embrace, we find our place.

Twilight whispers secrets there,
In the dusk, our spirits share.
With the goddess by our side,
In her light, forever abide.

## Nighttime Tides of Imagination

The moon whispers low, soft and bright,
Cradling dreams in the shroud of night.
Waves of thought crash on shores of the mind,
In the deep darkness, new worlds we find.

Stars twinkle like gems, scattered afar,
Guiding lost thoughts, like ships to a star.
The ocean of dreams lulls us to sleep,
As the tides of our wishes quietly sweep.

## Emblems of the Unseen Universe

In shadows thick, the mysteries unfold,
Secrets of life, whispered and told.
Patterns of existence, hidden in plain sight,
Emblems of truth bathed in pale moonlight.

Galaxies dance beyond our wild dreams,
Woven in stardust, bursting at the seams.
Connections uncharted, tethered with care,
In this unseen universe, we venture and dare.

## Moonbeam Serenades

In the stillness of night,
Soft whispers take flight.
Moonbeams paint the ground,
In silver, dreams are found.

Stars twinkle and sway,
Guiding the night's play.
Lunar songs so sweet,
Like shadows, they greet.

A symphony unfolds,
Where silence beholds.
Night's gentle embrace,
In darkness, we trace.

Under the celestial sky,
Time seems to fly.
Wrapped in tender glow,
Where soft secrets flow.

## Twilight Tranquility

As the sun bows low,
Colors start to flow.
A palette kissed by peace,
Where worries find release.

The horizon blushes bright,
Welcoming the night.
Birds sing their last song,
In twilight, we belong.

Gentle breezes breathe,
Through leaves, they weave.
Nature holds its breath,
Between life and death.

Shadows softly dance,
In this fleeting chance.
Time lingers with grace,
In twilight's warm embrace.

# Drowsy Glimmering Horizons

Where the sun meets the sea,
Drowsy waves whisper free.
Horizons softly gleam,
In the light of a dream.

Clouds drift, slow and wide,
On the ocean's tide.
Every sparkle sings,
Of the peace it brings.

The day fades away,
With hues of decay.
Gentle twilight sighs,
As the bright sun dies.

Night's blanket unfolds,
With its secrets untold.
Stars awaken to play,
In the glow of decay.

## When the Universe Whispers

In the hush of night,
Galaxies take flight.
Whispers soft and clear,
Echoing what we hear.

The cosmos breathes slow,
In a cosmic flow.
Secrets intertwined,
Journeying through the mind.

Stars share their delight,
In the velvet night.
Every twinkle's call,
Is a dream for us all.

When silence prevails,
And the starlight sails,
The universe sighs,
With a million replies.

# Embracing the Cosmic Night

In silence deep, the stars do gleam,
Whispers of night, a cosmic dream.
Galaxies twirl in velvet skies,
As we gaze up with wonderous eyes.

Waves of darkness cradle our fate,
In the vastness, we find our gate.
With stardust hearts, we drift and sway,
In the arms of night, we choose to stay.

Planets dance in a rhythmic trance,
Inviting our souls to join the dance.
The moonlight glows, a soft embrace,
Guiding us through this endless space.

Together we forge a path unknown,
In the mystery of night, we have grown.
Embracing the vast, the dark, the bright,
We find our home in the cosmic night.

## Cradled by Cosmic Light

Under a canopy of stars, we rest,
In the glow of the cosmos, we're blessed.
Soft beams wrap 'round us, warm and tight,
Cradled gently in cosmic light.

Nebulas swirl in hues so bright,
Painting our dreams with celestial sight.
Each shimmer a promise, pure delight,
Guiding our hearts through the night.

As comets dart past, we hold our breath,
Touched by the magic, we dance with death.
In the embrace of the universe's might,
We find our peace, cradled, upright.

Through galaxies wide, our spirit takes flight,
With every heartbeat, we chase the light.
In this moment, everything feels right,
Forever cradled by cosmic light.

# Dreaming Among the Stars

In the stillness of night, we dream,
Among the stars, we hear them beam.
Thoughts like comets streak so far,
As we drift softly, near and far.

Galaxies whisper secrets untold,
As our imaginations begin to unfold.
In the vastness, we weave our own lore,
Dreaming of worlds we've never explored.

With every twinkle, a tale takes shape,
In the cosmos' arms, we find escape.
The canvas of night, both vast and wide,
Holds our dreams, where we can abide.

Together, we linger, caught in this dance,
In the glow of the stars, we find our chance.
Leaving behind all worries and scars,
We are but dreams among the stars.

## Slumbering in Celestial Hues

Veils of twilight wrap around tight,
In slumber's grasp, we find our light.
Crimson and azure, the colors blend,
As we drift deeper, our hearts suspend.

Each hue a whisper, soft and sweet,
In cosmic dreams, our minds repeat.
The universe sings in tranquil tones,
As we rest gently on astral thrones.

The night sky glimmers, a vibrant hue,
Painting our dreams in shades anew.
Unraveling time, we float and muse,
In the embrace of these celestial hues.

Lost in the magic, we sigh and sway,
As starlight guides us, lighting the way.
Slumbering softly, we find our cues,
In the endless night, with celestial hues.

## Dreams Adrift on Shimmering Waves

Waves whisper softly to the shore,
Carrying dreams from nights before.
Shimmering light dances on the sea,
A tranquil heart, wild and free.

Golden horizons beckon the day,
Guiding lost dreams along the way.
Each ripple sings a soft, sweet tune,
Embracing all beneath the moon.

Voices of the ocean call my name,
In endless tides, I seek my flame.
Stars above reflect the light below,
In the depths, a world we sow.

As twilight drapes its velvet shawl,
I lose myself, then hear the call.
With every wave that gently breaks,
The journey of the heart awakes.

# The Night's Gentle Lullaby

Moonlight weaves through the trees,
A soothing song upon the breeze.
Stars twinkle like dreams in flight,
As the world embraces night.

Crickets hum their soft refrain,
Whispering secrets of the rain.
Each note cradles the weary soul,
In darkness, hearts become whole.

The sky unfolds a velvet dome,
A starry quilt that feels like home.
Clouds drift by with whispered grace,
In this calm, we find our place.

Wrapped in shadows, we drift away,
Held by the night, we softly sway.
In this lullaby's sweet embrace,
We find peace in time and space.

## Midnight Starlight Reverie

In the stillness of the night,
Starlight casts a golden light.
Dreams unspool like threads of silk,
Soft as shadows, pure as milk.

Whispers dance on the evening air,
Carrying wishes, light as prayer.
Each glimmer holds a hidden tale,
Guiding wanderers through the veil.

Velvet skies, deep and wide,
Hiding secrets that coincide.
In this realm where time stands still,
Hearts find comfort, dreams fulfill.

Beneath the vast, celestial dome,
Each star beckons, calling us home.
In midnight's arms, the world feels right,
Lost in reverie, wrapped in night.

## Celestial Calm

In twilight's hush, the stars ignite,
A canvas painted with pure light.
Softly glowing in the dark,
Each twinkle inspires a spark.

The universe breathes a gentle sigh,
Whispers of wonder float on by.
In silence, hearts begin to soar,
Opening pathways to explore.

Galaxies dance in tranquil grace,
Inviting us to join the chase.
With every pulse, we feel the flow,
In cosmic waves, our spirits grow.

Amidst the vast celestial sea,
We find the peace that sets us free.
In the calm, our souls align,
United with the stars' design.

## Cradles of Sleight and Spell

In shadows deep, whispers weave,
Crafting tales that hearts believe.
Softly glimmering, secrets unfold,
In a dance of wonder, stories told.

Winds of magic, gently sigh,
Stars above, they flicker and fly.
Cradles hold dreams, tender and light,
Guiding souls through the soft night.

Elusive paths where spirits glide,
Cradles of charm where hopes abide.
With every glance, enchantments flow,
In these realms, both fast and slow.

As twilight wraps its velvet cloak,
The world awakens, yet words remain broke.
In blissful reverie, we softly dwell,
In cradles of sleight and spell.

# Twilight Dreams in Twilight's Care

Beneath the stars, whispers sail,
Crafting dreams on a moonlit trail.
Twilight's embrace, a soothing balm,
In its cradle, the night feels calm.

Glistening shadows begin to play,
Chasing the remnants of the day.
Each dream a petal, soft and rare,
In twilight's arms, every thought laid bare.

Night unfolds with a gentle sigh,
As dreams take flight, we learn to fly.
Stars twinkle softly, guiding our way,
In twilight's care, we long to stay.

Amidst the hush, time begins to bend,
Where dreams and night together blend.
In this sacred space, hearts declare,
The beauty of twilight's gentle care.

## Rhythms of Starlight's Caress

In the vast expanse, silence sings,
Rhythms of night spread ethereal wings.
Starlight dances upon the sea,
Calling the lost, setting them free.

A gentle echo, a heartbeat's call,
In the embrace of night, we find our all.
Each twinkling star, a story holds,
In the cosmic weave, a dream unfolds.

Slowly we gather, in shadows deep,
Where starlight whispers and secrets keep.
In the glow, our fears laid to rest,
Eternal rhythms, we are blessed.

Underneath the celestial dome,
In starlight's caress, we find our home.
Every heartbeat, a shared delight,
We dance to the tune of the soft night.

# Celestial Harbor of Gentle Slumber

In the harbor where dreams dock tight,
Gentle slumber drapes its light.
Stars float softly on silken streams,
Cradling hearts in tender dreams.

A lullaby sung by the night breeze,
Washes over like whispered seas.
In this sanctuary, worries fade,
As night unveils its tranquil shade.

With every breath, the world slows down,
In celestial arms, we lose our frown.
A timeless moment where peace is found,
In slumber's embrace, we are unbound.

Through realms of wonder, we gently glide,
In the harbor of night, our hopes abide.
With gentle whispers, the universe calls,
To the celestial haven where quiet enthralls.

# Cosmic Cradle of Sleep

Stars weave dreams in the night,
Cradled soft in cosmic light.
Galaxies spin in quiet grace,
As time slows in this sacred space.

Moonbeams touch the ears of dawn,
Whispers of night begin to yawn.
The universe hums a lullaby,
As stardust dances on the sly.

In this cradle, souls do rest,
Floating gently, feeling blessed.
Waves of calm wash over me,
In the vastness, I'm truly free.

Sleep envelops in gentle shrouds,
While the dark sky wears its clouds.
Each secret spark softly gleams,
In the cradle of our dreams.

## Shimmering Nebula Nights

Nebulae glow in distant skies,
Colors blend with gentle sighs.
Stars ignite like distant fires,
Filling hearts with dreamer's desires.

Cosmic winds sweep through the dark,
Painting worlds with every spark.
In the silence, whispers flow,
Through the vast, where wonders grow.

Dust of ages, swirling bright,
Guiding souls through endless night.
Each twinkle tells a tale anew,
In the shimmering, endless blue.

Here we find our silent truth,
In the beauty of eternal youth.
Caught in the dance of time's embrace,
In the nebula's warm space.

## Hushed Moonlit Musings

Underneath the tender moon,
Thoughts take flight, a whispered tune.
Gentle breezes kiss the trees,
Carrying the night's soft pleas.

Stars above begin to hum,
A symphony of night's sweet drum.
In the quiet, dreams ignite,
Guiding hearts through veils of light.

Each reflection whispers dear,
Echoes of the night we hear.
In this hush, the soul takes flight,
Embracing all that feels so right.

Time drifts softly, like a stream,
In the moonlight's tender dream.
Moments linger, senses bloom,
In the magic of the room.

## Dusk's Embrace

Amber skies begin to fade,
As the light of day is laid.
Shadows stretch and softly creep,
In the stillness, promises keep.

Whispers of the day now rest,
In twilight's arms, we are blessed.
Colors blend, a soft caress,
In this moment, we find excess.

The horizon holds a secret hue,
As darkness dances with the dew.
Silence blankets all we know,
In the dusk, a gentle glow.

Here we pause, our hearts align,
In the waning light that shines.
Together held in evening's grace,
Forever caught in dusk's embrace.

## Shadows of the Midnight Realm

Whispers dance in moonlit air,
Darkened corners hold their stare.
Secrets veiled in twilight's shroud,
Echoes of the night, uncowed.

Figures flicker, shapes unfold,
Tales of dreams and hearts so bold.
Silent paths where shadows creep,
In the night, the silence deep.

Stars are winks from worlds afar,
Guiding souls like a distant star.
In the realm where whispers blend,
Time and space begin to bend.

Beneath the veil of midnight's lure,
Hearts beat fast, and spirits pure.
In the dance of shadows' grace,
We embrace the hidden space.

## Beneath the Gaze of the Night Sky

Underneath the vast expanse,
Stars ignite, in silence they dance.
Every glow a story told,
Dreams of silver, wishes bold.

With every twinkle, hopes arise,
Mirrors of the endless skies.
Beneath this dome, we stand as one,
Chasing shadows 'til the dawn.

Galaxies in silent flight,
Whirling in the velvet night.
Boundless journeys lie ahead,
Within the sky, our spirits tread.

In this moment, time stands still,
Hearts entwined with cosmic thrill.
Underneath the night's embrace,
We discover our rightful place.

## The Gentle Sway of Dream's Vessel

Drifting softly on the sea,
Where dreams arise, and spirits free.
Gentle waves that kiss the shore,
In the night, we yearn for more.

Moonlight dances on the tide,
In this boat, our fears collide.
Every whisper, every sigh,
Guides us through the starry sky.

With every murmur of the breeze,
We find solace, hearts at ease.
Together, we explore the night,
In the shadows, hearts take flight.

As we sail through realms unseen,
Through the fabric of the dream.
Each embrace, a sweetest spell,
In this vessel, all is well.

# An Odyssey Across the Sleeping Cosmos

In the realm where stardust plays,
Embarking on a journey's phase.
Through the void, our spirits soar,
Chasing wonders, evermore.

Galaxies spin in silent grace,
We navigate this endless space.
Comets trail with vivid light,
Guiding us through endless night.

Stepping lightly on cosmic strands,
Grasping dreams with tender hands.
Through the realms of time we glide,
On this journey, side by side.

As the universe unfolds wide,
In its depths, we will abide.
An odyssey that knows no end,
In this journey, love transcends.

# Beneath a Canopy of Glimmers

Stars twinkle bright above,
Whispers of dreams unfold.
The night wraps us in light,
Magic in stories told.

With every breath we take,
The world begins to sway.
Moonlight dances gently,
In twilight's soft ballet.

Branches weave their shadows,
Over fields of silver dew.
Nature holds her secrets,
In a sky so deep and blue.

Underneath the vastness,
We find what hearts can feel.
Beneath this canopy,
Our wishes become real.

## Sleepy Whispers in Twilight

The sun dips low with grace,
As colors start to blend.
Gentle sighs of twilight,
A soothing, calm ascent.

Crickets sing their sweet song,
Fading light, a soft embrace.
Day gives way to night's hush,
In this quiet, sacred space.

Shadows stretch and linger,
Painting dreams in soft hues.
As the world falls asleep,
We find moments to choose.

With each breath we gather,
The peace of dusk's retreat.
Sleepy whispers beckon us,
To the night we greet.

## Constellation Cradle

In the vastness overhead,
Stars weave tales of the past.
Shooting lights across the sky,
Moments too bright to last.

The Milky Way shines softly,
A river of dreams and light.
Each star a wish unspoken,
Guiding travelers tonight.

Galaxies of wonder,
Spin in a cosmic dance.
We cradle hope in starlight,
Embracing every chance.

Under this constellation,
Hearts beckon to align.
In the cradle of the night,
We find love that is divine.

## Nocturnal Echoes of Wonder

The night sings soft and low,
Echoes dance on the breeze.
A chorus of forgotten dreams,
Whispers through the trees.

Owls call with wisdom deep,
As shadows stretch and flow.
Each rustle holds a secret,
In the moon's soft, silver glow.

Stars appear like fireflies,
Lighting paths of the night.
Every glance a memory,
Held within starlit sight.

In this realm of wonder,
We explore the unseen.
Nocturnal echoes guide us,
To where our hearts have been.

## Celestial Harmony of Soft Slumber

Stars work their gentle glow,
Whispering dreams in silent flow.
Moonlight wraps the world so tight,
Guiding us through the tender night.

Clouds drift in a soft ballet,
Waltzing through the skies so gray.
Every sigh a lullaby,
Cradled by the night's sweet sigh.

Crickets serenade with glee,
Nature's hymn, a symphony.
In this peace, our hearts align,
Finding solace, pure, divine.

Wrapped in warmth, the shadows play,
As night unfolds, we drift away.
The universe, a tranquil sea,
Holds us close in harmony.

# Unraveling the Fabric of Night

Threads of darkness intertwine,
As stars begin their dance divine.
Nebulas whisper tales of old,
In silence, cosmic wonders unfold.

A tapestry of cosmic dreams,
Woven with celestial beams.
Every twinkle holds a spark,
Unraveling secrets from the dark.

Galaxies spin in gentle grace,
A timeless waltz through endless space.
The vast expanse, a velvet night,
Enfolds us in its tender light.

Through the silence, echoes hum,
As distant worlds beat like a drum.
Each moment blends with cosmic flow,
Unraveling pathways we long to know.

# The Sweet Cradle of the Milky Sky

In the cradle of the night,
Stars gather, a dazzling sight.
Galaxies swirl with gentle grace,
Painting dreams across the space.

The Milky Way, a ribbon bright,
Leads us through the cosmic light.
Planets whisper tales untold,
Secrets of the universe unfold.

Comets blaze a fleeting trail,
While the moon casts dreams that sail.
In this expanse, our spirits soar,
Cradled softly forevermore.

Beneath the night, we find our place,
Within the cosmos' warm embrace.
The sweet lull of the stars above,
Wrapped in night, we dream of love.

## Dances of Light in Evening's Embrace

As day surrenders to the night,
Colors fade, and dreams take flight.
Softly, stars begin to prance,
In a cosmic, twinkling dance.

Moonlit beams, a silken thread,
Guide our thoughts as we drift ahead.
Whispers of the night are sweet,
A lullaby for weary feet.

In shadows deep, the magic weaves,
As twilight gathers, the heart believes.
A gentle breeze begins to sway,
Embracing us 'til break of day.

In evening's arms, we lose our fears,
Surrounded by the light of years.
Dancing softly with the stars,
We find our peace, no matter where we are.

## Reveries Beneath the Astral Canopy

Beneath the stars, the night unfolds,
Whispers of dreams, stories untold.
In twilight's embrace, we drift and sway,
Lost in the magic of the Milky Way.

Comets dance through the velvet sky,
Painting tales where wishes lie.
The moonlight casts a gentle glow,
An ethereal path where hopes can flow.

From cosmic heights, our thoughts take flight,
Bathed in wonder, hearts feel light.
As galaxies swirl in a cosmic sea,
We weave our dreams, forever free.

In stillness, we find the night's soft peace,
Under the stars, all worries cease.
With each heartbeat, the universe sings,
In reverie, we unfurl our wings.

## Stardust Dreams in Moonlit Fields

In fields of silver, soft and wide,
We lie beneath the celestial tide.
With starlit whispers in the breeze,
Dreams take shape among the trees.

The moon beams down with a tender kiss,
Inviting us into the realm of bliss.
Each glimmering star, a wish upon,
In this sacred space, we carry on.

As twilight hums a lullaby sweet,
Our hearts sync with the starlit beat.
In the hush of night, we close our eyes,
To find our fate among the skies.

The cosmos cradles us, warm and kind,
With dreams of stardust intertwining our mind.
In moonlit fields, we find our way,
Guided by hope, till break of day.

## Bedtime Ballads of the Cosmos

As night descends, the stars ignite,
A lullaby sings of distant light.
Each note a spark, a stellar gleam,
Wrapped in the warmth of a cosmic dream.

The galaxies swirl in hushed delight,
While comets race through the endless night.
Their tales of wonder and age-old lore,
Whispered softly from shore to shore.

In the embrace of the twilight realm,
The universe guides, we gently helm.
With every heartbeat, a song is spun,
In the symphony of the moon and sun.

So let your worries drift afar,
As you dance beneath a shooting star.
The cosmos wraps us in gentle charms,
With bedtime ballads, safe in its arms.

# The Lull Before the Dawn

In the hush of night, the world takes pause,
Wrapped in slumber, lost in applause.
The stars gently fade, a whisper's breath,
Beyond the horizon, awaits the depth.

The sky blushes soft, a tender glow,
As dreams weave tales of the night's tableau.
Moments suspended in a silent trance,
As the cosmos hums its tranquil dance.

The moon nods off, the sun peeks through,
Painting the world in a golden hue.
With every breath, we find our place,
In the lull before daybreak's embrace.

So hold this moment, tender and bright,
For dawn brings forth the gift of light.
In the still of night, let your heart fawn,
For beauty lies in the lull before dawn.

# Stars in a Sleepy Sea

Stars are dancing on the tide,
Whispers of the night abide.
Glowing dreams in waters deep,
Cradled by the sea's soft sweep.

Moonlight paints the waves with grace,
Encircling night in a warm embrace.
Gentle currents, soft and slow,
Guiding hearts where dreams can go.

Portals open wide and clear,
Filling skies with all we hear.
Rocking boats in lullabies,
Underneath these velvet skies.

Sleepy stars will softly gleam,
We wander through this tranquil dream.
In a world where wishes flow,
Stars will light the paths we know.

## Astral Adventures of the Mind

In the cosmos, thoughts take flight,
Dancing through the endless night.
Galaxies of dreams unfold,
Stories waiting to be told.

Time dissolves, reality bends,
Every thought a journey sends.
Floating free on stardust beams,
Chasing ever-brightest dreams.

Echoes of the universe call,
In the silence, we feel small.
Yet within, the spirit grows,
Seeking paths nobody knows.

Nebulas of vibrant hue,
Paint the mind with visions new.
Astral travels, hearts aligned,
In this vast expanse, we find.

## Celestial Daze and Midnight Haze

In twilight's arms, the stars ignite,
Whispers float in the soft night light.
Celestial daze, a gentle trance,
Guiding dreams in cosmic dance.

Midnight haze wraps the world in peace,
As shadows wane, and worries cease.
Moonbeams kiss the earth below,
In silent night, our spirits glow.

Every star a spark of grace,
Whirling through the vastness of space.
The sky's a canvas, deep and wide,
Where hopes and dreams dutifully ride.

In the stillness, magic sings,
Beneath the stars, the heart takes wings.
In this space where time blurs fast,
We find our dreams, and peace at last.

## Luminescent Dreams Unfold

In the quiet, visions glow,
Whispers of what we do not know.
Luminescent dreams arise,
Painting colors in the skies.

Floating softly through the night,
Chasing shadows, seeking light.
Heartbeats echo in the dark,
Every pulse a lasting spark.

In this realm where wonders weave,
Infinite tales our minds conceive.
Magic lingers in the air,
Orbs of light, a bright affair.

With each thought, the world expands,
Boundless journeys, endless lands.
Together, through these dreams, we soar,
Luminescence opens every door.

### Dreams in Celestial Hues

In twilight's embrace, colors blend,
Soft whispers of light, as day starts to end.
The canvas above, painted bright,
Awakens our souls in the gentle night.

Wonders unfurl in shades of blue,
Each star a story, waiting for you.
With every wish cast into the sky,
Dreams take flight, like birds that fly.

The horizon glows with a golden kiss,
Moments like these, we simply can't miss.
In silence we drift, hearts open wide,
As dreams swirl softly, on starlit tide.

Together we'll dance, amid cosmic glee,
In dreams of the universe, forever free.
For in these hues, our spirits play,
Guided by stars, we'll find our way.

## Whispers of the Cosmic Night

Beneath the cosmos, whispers take flight,
Melodies drift in the still of the night.
The universe hums a soft, sweet tune,
As hearts beat gently beneath the moon.

Galaxies swirl in a waltz so divine,
Each twinkle a secret in shadow and shine.
Listen closely, for echoes abound,
In the lull of the night, magic is found.

Stardust collects on dreams yet to wake,
A tapestry woven with each choice we make.
In the silence, a promise rings clear,
That love is the language we all long to hear.

Float with me now, let worries subside,
In whispers and dreams, let our souls collide.
Together we'll travel, through vastness so wide,
In the cosmic night, we'll always abide.

## The Moon's Lullaby

Cradled in silver, the moon softly sings,
A lullaby woven from the night's gentle wings.
Her light spills softly on slumbering land,
Caressing the dreams that awaken at hand.

In the hush of the night, worries all cease,
The moon spreads her glow, wrapping all in peace.
Under her watchful gaze, shadows retreat,
As starlight dances, with rhythm and beat.

Each note she whispers, a promise of hope,
Guiding us gently on this tightrope.
Nestled in beams, our hearts start to sway,
The moon's lullaby beckons, leading the way.

So close your tired eyes, let your spirit soar,
In the depths of her song, you will find more.
A celestial embrace in the nighttime's stillness,
The moon's tender touch brings infinite chillness.

## Starlit Dreams and Velvet Nights

In velvet nights beneath the vast sky,
Where starlit dreams begin to fly.
Each twinkle a wish, whispered with care,
In the stillness of night, magic fills the air.

The cosmos unfolds, a tapestry bright,
Guiding lost souls with its shimmering light.
Soft melodies cling to the breeze's flight,
As we wander through dreams, in pure delight.

Hand in hand beneath the celestial dome,
In starlit paths, we find our home.
Together we dance where the shadows play,
Embraced by the night, we're swept away.

Each moment a treasure, in softest embrace,
Time stands still, in this sacred space.
In starlit dreams, our hearts intertwine,
Velvet nights whisper, forever you're mine.

# A Symphony of Soft Stardust

In the night sky, whispers play,
Soft stardust dances, leading the way.
Crickets sing their lullabies,
Under the watchful moonlit eyes.

Gentle breezes sweep the glade,
Where shadows of dreams are softly made.
Echoes of wishes linger near,
Wrapped in the warmth of starry cheer.

Glowing embers in the vast expanse,
Each twinkle invites a cosmic dance.
A symphony of night unfolds,
Stories untold in starlight's hold.

With every heartbeat, the cosmos sighs,
As we drift among the midnight skies.
In the silence, magic we find,
A song of stardust, love intertwined.

## Celestial Embrace at Dusk

As the sun dips low in grace,
The stars emerge, a tender lace.
Whispers of night begin to weave,
A celestial embrace, as we believe.

The horizon blushes, painted gold,
Secrets of twilight quietly told.
Moonbeams gather, a soft caress,
In this moment, we find our rest.

Night wraps us in its velvet arms,
While cosmic wonders cast their charms.
A symphony of silence is spun,
In the peaceful glow of day undone.

Together we gaze, hearts aligned,
In this tranquil space, solace we find.
Celestial tales in starlight blend,
As night's embrace whispers, "Time shall suspend."

## Silhouettes of Slumbering Stars

In the tapestry of night, they lie,
Silhouettes of stars, quietly high.
Softly flickering, as dreams unfold,
In their gaze, secrets of old.

Wrapped in shadows, they softly gleam,
Guiding us softly through the dream.
Each twinkle a whisper, a beckoning cry,
In stillness, we soar, we drift, we fly.

Lying in silence, the world fades away,
A canvas of night, where wishes play.
The universe sways with a gentle tune,
As slumbering stars hold the night in bloom.

In the heart of the dark, they alight,
Painting our dreams with silver light.
Silhouettes whisper the stories they know,
As the night cradles us, soft and slow.

## Night's Canvas of Dreams

Under a canopy of silken night,
Dreams are painted in colors bright.
With starlit brushes, the universe schemes,
Creating a canvas where hope redeems.

Violet hues blend with midnight blue,
A swirling design, both old and new.
Each dream a stroke, delicate and fine,
In the gallery of thoughts, they intertwine.

As shadows dance upon the ground,
In every corner, magic is found.
The breeze carries secrets, old and wise,
While night blooms open beneath dark skies.

Holding our hearts in tender embrace,
We wander through this enchanted space.
Night's canvas whispers what dreams can be,
A palette of stars, forever free.

## Slumber Beneath the Brighter Stars

In twilight's grasp, the world drifts low,
Soft whispers dance where cool winds blow.
Dreamers gather with eyes closed tight,
Under the watch of the sparkling night.

The constellations twinkle above,
Painting the skies with tales of love.
Stars like lanterns, guiding our way,
Into the dreams where shadows play.

Crickets sing a lullaby sweet,
As slumber wraps us in its sheet.
Night's gentle hand, a tender embrace,
Cradling us in this sacred space.

Beneath the blanket of midnight's hue,
We find our peace, both old and new.
In dreams we wander, far and free,
In slumber's realm, just you and me.

# Moonbeam Melodies

Under the moon's enchanting gaze,
Soft melodies drift in a gentle haze.
Notes cascade like silvery streams,
Awakening all our sweetest dreams.

The nightingale sings to the starry skies,
While shadows dance as the dawn denies.
Swaying softly with each note's flow,
Whispers of night in a silent glow.

Each beam a story, a tale untold,
Bathed in silver, both bright and bold.
Ethereal strains that the heart can feel,
In moonlight's warmth, our spirits heal.

As twilight fades and darkness clears,
We find our solace, setting fears.
With every rhythm, our souls align,
In moonbeam melodies, love divine.

## Sails of Sleep on Heavenly Seas

Drifting softly on twilight's tide,
Sails of sleep in the night abide.
Gentle waves cradle dreams so deep,
Upon this journey, we gently sweep.

Stars are the lanterns guiding our way,
As we voyage through night into day.
In whispers of winds, secrets we keep,
Riding the currents of peaceful sleep.

Clouds like pillows, soft and white,
Hold our thoughts in the velvet night.
Setting our sails with a breath of ease,
Exploring the vastness of heavenly seas.

With every sway, our worries release,
Finding comfort in infinite peace.
Together we drift, where all is fair,
In dreams' embrace, without a care.

# Moonlit Tranquility

In the hush of night, a serene glow,
Moonlit paths where soft breezes flow.
Every shadow whispers a tale,
In tranquil moments, we gently sail.

Stars like diamonds in velvet skies,
Cradle our thoughts as the silence sighs.
With every breath, we find our grace,
In moonlit stillness, a warm embrace.

Nature's lullaby sings so sweet,
Cultivating calm where hearts can meet.
In the quietude, our spirits entwine,
Wrapped in the magic, so pure, divine.

Each moment stretches, time stands still,
In moonlit tranquility, we feel the thrill.
As dreams cascade like the gentle tide,
In peaceful shadows, forever abide.